MY 50TH NAVIGATION

AROUND THE WORLD OF WORDS

NAILA RAIS

ISBN 979-888530775-8

ONE THING I WILL EVER CHOOSE WAS THE
MOTIVATION OF MY FAMILY.

I whole heartedly dedicate my book to my parents Mr Rais Beg
and Mrs Mahar Afshan along with my family, specially Qudsia
ma'am. I pay humble thanks to my freinds for being too
supported. My gratitude goes to Notion Press fot publishing
the book.

Contents

Foreword

The title of this book of poems, My 50th Navigation not only talks about love, but it also contains motivational poetries. Yes, The composition of a poem is the manifestation of feelings through thoughts via words onto paper, in other words, it is the conveyance of ordinary words into other, more poetic words, whilst the reader is confronted with the task to re-establish the origin of metaphoric references.

And here's one more way that poetry is like music. It's said that people's

favorite tune is the one most popular when they first fell seriously in

love—though probably everything surrounding such a moment remains

memorable. It has to do with what the heart is paying rapt attention

to. So too with poems. Our allegiances are formed by our first serious

readings—the poems we get by heart, as it were. I don't mean childhood

rhymes or classroom assignments

~ Naila Rais

Preface

Blazing at the gazing sky,

Deep into the heart as the beach comber rise,

Sitting and counting the glazing of the pebbles,

When near the seashore heart heaviness arise

    In the coil letter of her voice roll,

Up to the sky spreading with wind rode,

Like a funnel her soul cries,

Taking her cries to a heaven with a code

Acknowledgements

Ghosts freaks and goblins shouts
We met a traveler in the woods
Who went wherever his horse lay!

I want my readers to read the book till last to get the mystery solved. Here's an amazing list of poetries.

Prologue

I have a paper in my head

A pen in my heart

And words in my soul

Embedded with love and warmth

    But wrapped in shattered heap

    I have a rhythm in my mind

A tune in my veins

And lyric in my mouth

Embedded with fun and chorus

    But wrapped in shattered heap

    I have craziness in my nerve

A view in my eyes

And a image in my cerebrum

Embedded with colors and designs

    But wrapped in shattered heap

1. War Hero

At dawn, in a stuffy and smoky carriage,
A bulky woman in deep mourning,
Behind her puffing and mourning her husband
A tiny man, thin and weakly, his face death
white
Now, if one dies young and happy,
Without having seen ugly sides of life,
The boredom of it, the petiness, the bitterness of
disillusion,
At least thank God, as I (passenger)do
My son died in the best way he could,
The reason, I don't wear mourning,
He shook his light fawn coat so as to,
After he ended with a smile of sob
His eyes were watery, his livid lips tremble,
Quiet so, quiet so, agreed the other,
The woman who bundled under her coat,
Listened and listened and cried
But, something that might show her,
A mother should resign herself to send her son,
Not even to death but to a probably a dangerous
As by her grief had been greater that nobody,
could share her feelings

But the words of a traveler amazed,
She herself was wrong who couldn't rise,
To the height of those fathers and mothers to
resign,
Not only to the departure of their son but even to
their death
It seemed for her, she had stumbled intoa world,
A world so far unknown,
Then suddenly just as if she heard nothing she
asked,
Then is your only son really dead?
Broke into harrowing, heart-rending,
uncontrollable sobs.

2. Be My Light

O' Allah help me
O' Allah guide me
Let me come out of vain
Let me vanish my pain.
O' Allah listen to my prayers
O' Allah listen to my prayers
I obey you and pray
Guide me the way of truth
Forgive me for my ignorance
And take hold of my actions
O' Allah shower mercy on sinful me.
O' Allah listen to my prayers
O' Allah listen to my prayers
My head on ground
My hands open for dua
Guide me the way of peace
Consider my goodness of sinful me.
O' Allah listen to my prayers
O' Allah listen to my prayers!

3. Beauty Of The Supreme Power

The heart may break
The words may die
The voice will crack
The tears will dry
And the king of king
Will shower his mercy
The world may turn upside down
The hope may get shattered
The body will faint
The time will matter
And the king of king
Will shower his mercy
The friends may turn into foe
The soul may feel lonely
The eyes will widen
The inner voice will shout
And the king of king
Will shower his mercy.

4. Bewilder Heart

When all the dentils of her sorrows
Were fragmented into shallow sobs
And hovering darkness depressing her dreams
To trover all happiness gone.
In the misty, on the foggy night
Beside the demos on the countryside
She calls the prayer of her unsaid words
But who cares about her silent screams.

5. Blossoms Of The Spring

The aroma of the flowers,
The breeze for the hours;
The sunshine on the face,
The natures beauty is the base;
Welcome's the new glory,
Of the little leaves;
Scattered all around,
The golden coins in heaps;
All animals are singing,
Reminding of the spring,
Sunshine singing the hymn;
Cherish of the earth,
Celebrating Glory's birth;
Chirping of the birds,
Makes the beauty lurd;
Buzzing of the bees,
Tides in the seas;
Insects makes the sound,
The spring is all around;
The water flows,
The air blows;
The little green saplings,
Shines with glow;

The spring has come,

With the memories some;

Lets have fun,

In the happy sun....

Live a happy life

Never make it a hive

Just keep smiling

As the moments are shining.

6. Busy In Their Mobile Goad

Little flowers of today are much more dickier,

B'coz of inebriation of fast food filled in,

They abjure all outdoor play,

Busy in their mobile goad.

Today they are inimical instead of happier,

B'coz of stubbornness in their mood filled in,

They abjure all gaff play,

Busy in their mobile goad.

If they deduce to alacrity of gaining, they'll go higher,

B'coz of mirth of rave filled in,

Busy in their feisty goad.

Today they should be beguile,

B'coz of innocence of youth filled in,

But they abjure all byous play,

Busy in their mobile goad.

Call Me Above

Oh! Let me come out

No more I can bear

I have chronic pain in my heart

And a great deep piece

Oh! Let me forget

B'coz as I use to think
I'm left unconscious
And a statue rare still
O'Thou call me above
Faraway in the heaven land
I'm left alone
As a bare tree...
O' Thou grant me one wish
Take me in your hand
This world is of no use
And cruelty is deep rooted here

7. Can't Bid You Adieu

You are higher than the sky
Taller than the spiritual mountains
Far beyond the depth of seas
With the depth of empathy.
Your kindness fly high and high
With the leaflets of motivation
Filled in loads of love and joy
Making us feel proud for being your student

8. Childhood Memories

Years by years innocence change
But the memories never fade
From the lightning and cheers of the dawn
Till the setting sun of dusk
The plays we all had
The fights we all did
The day we ran down the road
The day we were Frightened
All have some deep piece
Beyond the horizon, floating in the
Seas...
As the days goes by
The keen for butterfly gets over
From the mountains to the valley
The wind blows and blows
The tapping of the feet in water
Or the cries all day
Have now been a memory
Of the happy golden hours
And the quest for rainbow and sun
Now is all done and gone forever

9. Christmas Eve

Jingling bells twinkling stars all around
Lightning lamps, glazing bulb far above
Ye! Ye!
Santa Claus is coming on the ride
Ye! Ye!
Jumping and dancing, children running clapping
all around
Jingling bells, twinkling stars all around
Carols singing, Xmas tree swinging
Ye! Ye!
Laughter of children on merry go round
Santa Claus is hugging and spreading gifts
Ye! Ye!
With whistling all around
Ye! Ye!

10. Dear, Pole Star

Twinkle twinkle burning ball
Tell me the way to you
Faraway from the earth
Sparking in the faraway land.
Pointing north to the traveler
In the desert during nights
Oh! Tell me please I will come to you
With invitation to my birthday party.

11. Death Is Solution

On the barren, thorny land
Waiting for my eternity in the graveyard
I sit alone crying and thinking
Why don't people forget when I have changed
I have asked forgiveness from Almighty
Hitherto I was not concious at that time.
Kill me but don't defame me
Don't make fun of my innocence
One day I can be mature like you too
As time comes for everyone
But don't disclose my depression.
It rained heavily all light so long
Even there is flood in morning too
My pillow can never be draught
Happiness for broken soul can never be bought
And hatred I have always got
But yes! From all this my heart can stop! !

12. Fan Of Cricket, Junior Spinner

O' little crazy little boy

Why don't you play with any toy?

Great lover of funky ball

O'little bowler you are thin and tall

You sway your bat fiercely

And you get teased so sweetly

When you are unable to hit the ball

O'little boy it's not wide and tall

Sometimes you don't care if it's mouth or head

If it hurts, no! It's not bad

You are awesome boy with wicked rules

You get teased just with little clues

O'little crazy, little boy

To watch your game is real joy

You are great fan of cricket

Just to tease you we all shout it's wicket!

Wicket!!

13. Fragrance of you my love

Seeing your face I smell the roses
The fragrance of lilies and daisies
The eyes bow down, the face glitter
With the spark of diamonds
I can feel your pulses
Even at a long mile.
The moonlight shakes when its creep
At the dawn on your face
When you just stand and watch
And let my heart rest on your smile
I feel the warmth of you
But knew you are not mine.
The butterflies and birds flew by
The stream chatters on your kindness
Even at a busiest crowd
You come and raise my heartbeats
Feeling your presence my words failed
But you knew much better, silence sings I love
you.
My voice glow as the minutes pass
Yes you and I are thinking
Neither the present nor the future

But the past deep memories
Thinking of that day
When I and You were two unknown souls.
Every time I speak to you Dear
My words fail you just say
Nothing matters it just happens
And it makes my heart heavy
Thinking of that time
I regret why I left you alone.
I love you LOVE, love loves you so much
And I am jealous of the love
Although love loves in supernatural
And nature sings your prays
I care you but don't know if you too
Love me, care me, think of me to make love love
me.
Even respect comes and salutes you
For the golden heart you hold
But the world stills wait for you
To come and join their game
And to the wonder you didn't come
To rejoy but to raise my beats.
You are my love, no doubt you care
Even you take my name with pride
I just sit and watch you smile
From faraway and far behind
My eyes glow, my face shine

Feeling your presence for the sake of mine.

I Love you, you care for Me

I smile at you, you just joins

My eyes bow down, seeing your face

Even my voice cracks at you

And I feel warmth of you

But knew too much, YOU are not MINE.

14. I Go On Forever

Life goes tough, roads seem rough,
I went, I go, I go on forever
The boats sails, the idea fails,
I tried, I try, I try on forever
Eyes filled with tear, no one to hear
I cried, I cry, I cry on forever
When troubles fear, came a lovely dear,
I laughed, I laugh, I laugh on forever
I compromise, to keep my promise,
I made, I make, I make on forever
Society full of myth, I never agree with,
I broke, I break, I break on forever
I love you, you love me,
I thought, I think, I think on forever
The mountains shine, the opportunities line,
I jump, I jumped, I jumped on forever
I want to loose fur, as it never lure,
I threw, I throw, I throw on forever
The eyes closed, the breathing slows,
I live, I died, I died for forever
I bear pain, why pain always rain,
I bore, I bear, I bear on forever

Thank You

Dear Readers,

Thank you so much for reading my books. I know there are a lot of books out there, and it means a great deal to me that you picked up one of mine, and chose to spend time with characters I created. Ever since I was a little kid, I knew I wanted to be a writer, and having readers like you is a dream come true.

Love, Naila Rais